Hello, Family Members,

Learning to read is one of the most important accomplishments of early childhood. **Hello Reader!** books are designed to help children become skilled readers who like to read. Beginning readers learn to read by remembering frequently used words like "the," "is," and "and"; by using phonics skills to decode new words; and by interpreting picture and text clues. These books provide both the stories children enjoy and the structure they need to read fluently and independently. Here are suggestions for helping your child *before*, *during*, and *after* reading:

Before

- Look at the cover and pictures and have your child predict what the story is about.
- Read the story to your child.
- Encourage your child to chime in with familiar words and phrases.
- Echo read with your child by reading a line first and having your child read it after you do.

During

- Have your child think about a word he or she does not recognize right away. Provide hints such as "Let's see if we know the sounds" and "Have we read other words like this one?"
- Encourage your child to use phonics skills to sound out new words.
- Provide the word for your child when more assistance is needed so that he or she does not struggle and the experience of reading with you is a positive one.
- Encourage your child to have fun by reading with a lot of expression . . . like an actor!

After

- Have your child keep lists of interesting and favorite words.
- Encourage your child to read the books over and over again. Have him or her read to brothers, sisters, grandparents, and even teddy bears. Repeated readings develop confidence in young readers.
- Talk about the stories. Ask and answer questions. Share ideas about the funniest and most interesting characters and events in the stories.

I do hope that you and your child enjoy this book.

—Francie Alexander
Reading Specialist,
Scholastic's Learning Ventures

To Engineer Ann
— L.J.H.

For Betsy
— J.W.

ISBN 0-439-08757-0

Text copyright © 2000 by Lorraine Jean Hopping.
Illustrations copyright © 2000 by Jody Wheeler.
All rights reserved. Published by Scholastic Inc.
SCHOLASTIC, HELLO READER, CARTWHEEL BOOKS, and associated
logos are trademarks and/or registered trademarks of Scholastic Inc.

Library of Congress Cataloging-In-Publication Data
Hopping, Lorraine Jean.
    Wild Weather : floods! / by Lorraine Jean Hopping ; illustrated by Jody Wheeler.
        p.   cm.—(Hello reader! Science—Level 4)
    Summary: Describes the causes of floods, the devastation that they can cause, and ways to fight them.
        ISBN 0-439-08757-0
        [1. Floods—Juvenile Literature]   [1. Floods.] I. Wheeler, Jody, ill.
    II. Title.
    III. Hello science reader! Level 4.

GB1399.H66 2000
363.34'92—dc21
                                                                99-4041772

12   11   10   9   8   7   6   5   4   3   2   1   00   01   02   03   04   05   06

Printed in the U.S.A.   24
First printing, April 2000

Floods!

by Lorraine Jean Hopping
Illustrated by Jody Wheeler

Hello Reader! Science — Level 4

SCHOLASTIC INC. Cartwheel BOOKS®

New York   Toronto   London   Auckland   Sydney
Mexico City   New Delhi   Hong Kong

Chapter 1

River of Ice

No one was watching.
But on a spring night in Vermont,
a frozen river was cracking up.
Chunks of ice, like mini-icebergs,
floated in a bumpy jumble.
While people slept, the river of ice
gushed downstream.

Near dawn, the ice stopped at
a bridge near a town.
Chunks jammed up like cars
that cannot avoid an accident.
More ice streamed in.
The ice jam blocked the water
from flowing downstream.
By daybreak, the Winooski River
was rising fast.

People in downtown Montpelier
(mont-PEEL-yer) had no warning.
The river spilled out of its bed and
reached their doorsteps in minutes.
The flood trapped workers in the
top floors of stores and offices.

Now people were watching.
They saw water swallow cars,
parking meters, and fire hydrants.
A hot boiler exploded when the
cold water hit it.
The streets became muddy canals.

Rescuers used boats to take the
trapped people to safety.

Schools closed so that students could get out of the river's way. Instead, some children went downtown to watch the flood. "Too dangerous!" said rescuers. They told the children to go to high ground — *right now*.

The flood had not reached the library.
But in case it did, some children helped move their favorite books out of the basement.

For hours, the river seeped into higher parts of town.
To stop it, someone had to break up the ice jam.

Experts called engineers
(en-juh-NEERZ) had an idea.
They brought in a tall crane with a
pointy weight hanging from the top.
Over and over, the ball pounded
the ice, smashing holes in it.

At sunset, the ice jam broke open.
A burst of ice and water gushed
downstream.
It snapped a steel bridge in half!

Breaking the jam was like pulling
the plug in a swimming pool.
The river sank, allowing floodwater
to drain out of town.

Chapter 2

Jams, Dams, and Sand Bags

A flood is simply lots of water flowing into a dry area. Flooding can stretch over days. But a flash flood, such as the Vermont ice jam, takes minutes. Water can flow fast enough to fill a football stadium in seconds!

It is easy to picture how many
floods happen.
A dam breaks, and a lake gushes
forth in a hurry and a fury.
A tsunami (soo-NAH-mee),
or tall tidal wave, swamps a city.
A hurricane washes seawater
over a row of beach houses.

All floods happen for the same
reason: gravity.
Gravity pulls water down
from high ground to low ground.
The water does not flow in a line.
Instead, rivers snake across land
in twists and turns.

In the spring of 1993, rivers in the
Mississippi River Basin snaked out
of control. (See map.)
Weeks of rain filled the rivers up to
their banks — and higher.

THE MISSISSIPPI RIVER BASIN

Mississippi River
Missouri River
Minnesota
Wisconsin
Iowa
Illinois
Missouri
Gulf of Mexico

People from Minnesota to Missouri were worried.
People in the floodplains of those states were scared.
Floodplains are low, flat areas near a river.
They are the first and worst places that floodwaters swamp.

Children helped their families fill bags with sand.
People tossed millions of sandbags on top of levees (LEV-eez) to make them higher.
Levees are long, wide mounds of earth that hold rivers in place.

In most cities, levees did their job. But rivers broke through eight out of ten levees in the countryside.

Farm crops in the floodplains
quickly turned into muddy lakes.

The current, or moving water,
peeled the blacktop off of roads.
It swept chairs, sofas, beds, and
houses downstream.

On one farm, floodwater trapped
pigs on a barn roof for five days.

Rescuers picked up and carried
the pigs, one by one, into boats.

In Des Moines, Iowa, water flowed
all over town.
But there wasn't enough to drink.
The flood poured unsafe water into
the city drinking supply.

Floodwater took weeks to dry up
or to drain back into rivers.
When it did, thick mud and piles
of trash covered the floodplain.
One home owner said the mud
looked like chocolate pudding—
only it stank.

About forty people died in the
Great Flood of 1993.
Millions lost their homes.

Chapter 3

Soft and Dangerous

Have you ever felt soft raindrops
on your cheeks?
Water can be gentle.
But it can also be deadly, especially
during floods.

What makes water dangerous?
Water is very heavy, for one thing.
The water in a bathtub weighs as
much as six nine-year-olds!

Water moves, for another thing.
Heavy, moving objects have a lot
of power to push things around.

You can jog as fast as many rivers
flow.
Yet a knee-deep current can easily
sweep you off your feet.
A fast, knee-deep current can carry
a car downstream.
In fact, half of all flood deaths
happen to people in cars or trucks.

A swift river is dangerous.
But imagine what a speedy, fifteen-
story wall of water can do.
On May 31, 1889, many unlucky
people in Pennsylvania found out.

Rain was partly to blame.
It swelled the lake behind a dam.
But the dam was old and weak.

John Parke, an engineer, knew it.
On May 31, he hopped on a horse
to warn people in the town below.

"The dam is breaking!" John shouted. "Run for your life!"

The lake leaped through the weak dam in a giant wave.

Roaring water ripped up forests at the roots.
Trees popped high in the air like toothpicks.
The current scooped up all the soil as if peeling back a carpet.
It left only bare rock behind.

Two villages were wiped off the mountain.
Most of the city of Johnstown was smashed to splinters.

Six-year-old Gertrude Quinn ran
out of her house just before the
flood flattened it.
She and other people rode on a
floating mattress to safety.

More than two thousand people died
in that flood. It was the worst flood
in United States history.

Today, terrible floods still happen
all over the world.
But they kill fewer people.
Engineers and scientists have found
ways to save lives.

Chapter 4

An Engineer on Ice

Kate White is an engineer.
She studies ice jams like the one
in Vermont.
To see if a jam might break, Kate
has to walk on rivers of ice.

"The first time I did it, I was
scared," Kate says. "If the ice
cracks, I can fall into the river."

To be safe, Kate jabs the ice with
a pole to feel for weak spots.
When she can, Kate walks where
she has already stepped.
She knows those spots are strong
enough to support her weight.

Kate and a partner drill a hole
in the ice to see how thick it is.
Thick chunks of ice can turn a bad
flood into a worse one.

Kate also measures the speed
of the current.
But water depth is the most
important thing to know.

"Rising water means for us to get
off the ice — fast!" says Kate.
Rising water pushes hard on the ice
and can crack it open.
One time, Kate got off an ice jam
minutes before it broke!

Engineers use the ice data to stop
some jams from flooding.
They sprinkle black dust on the ice
to melt it.
Dark colors absorb sunlight well.

Engineers can blow up some jams.
The blast lets water flow freely
instead of building up behind a jam.

Even if engineers cannot prevent
a flood, they can warn people.

In January 1996, families in
Morrisonville, New York, were told
to go to higher ground.
An icy flood swept away many
of their houses, but no one died.

Like engineers, scientists also
predict floods and warn people.

They put up tall, sturdy pipes over
a wide area.
The pipes collect rain as it falls.
Lots of rain sets off an alarm signal.
The signal travels to scientists in
a city, who put out flood warnings.

Kate White uses an alarm, too.
She puts wires in the ice at the site
of a jam.
If the ice breaks, it snaps the wires
and sets off an alarm.
The alarm gives people downriver
time to move to high ground.

Like rainfall, too much snowfall
can cause flooding.
In early 1997, North Dakota and
Minnesota had more snow than
anyone had ever recorded.
In April, the snow melted fast.

Water tumbled down mountains.
The frozen soil below could not
soak up all the water.
Water rose and gushed over levees.
It poured into sewers, basements,
and, finally, whole houses.

Grand Forks, North Dakota,
was swamped.
But thanks to a flood warning
the town was empty.
Everyone had fled to safety.

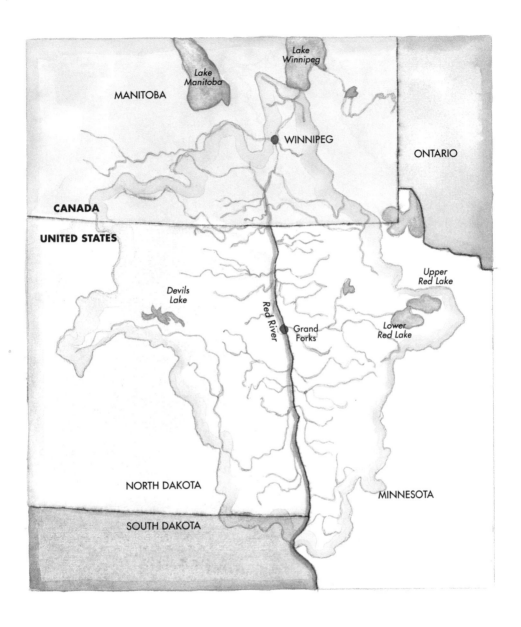

Chapter 5

Why Farmers Like Floods

Warnings, alarms, and levees help save lives.

But why do people live near rivers in the first place?

This may sound strange.

But many people live near rivers *because* of floods!

The Yellow River in China may be
the deadliest river in the world.
Its floods have killed millions
of people.
Yet millions more, mostly farmers,
choose to live on its banks.

Remember the "chocolate pudding"
left by floods?
That stinky mud has chemicals
that plants need to grow.
It turns floodplains into rich
farmland.
Rivers also provide water for both
crops and farmers.

Wildlife need floods, too.
Many plants and animals live
in wetlands such as swamps,
marshes, and riverbanks.

Wetlands often dry up.
Floods refill them with water.

At one time, the Colorado River
in the western United States
flooded often.
But people began to use too much
of the river's water.

By the 1990s, the river was just
a thin trickle in some places.
Many fish and river plants died.

In 1996, scientists flooded the
Colorado River on purpose.
They opened a dam and let water
roar down the river through the
Grand Canyon.

Scientists timed the water speed.
They measured the amount of mud
and rocks that the water carried.
They watched how the flood changed
the riverbed.

The experiment, scientists hoped,
might teach them how to bring
wildlife back to the canyon.
It might also teach them how to
control wild floods.

People in flood areas can fight
floods on their own.
They can build houses on stilts
or wooden posts, for example.
Stilts raise the houses above the
water level of a flood.

Every summer, heavy rains flood
the nation of Bangladesh, Asia.
Some people simply pack up and
move to high ground.
Then they return and rebuild
during the dry season.

Near the Yangtze (YANG-see) River
in China, people are planting more
trees.
Trees soak up water and help keep
floods from carrying away soil.

People will never live without
floods.
But many are learning to live
with floods.

Flood Safety Tips

- Know the way to higher ground. Go there during a flood warning.
- Don't play near levees or dry ditches.
- Always camp on high ground.
- Keep extra drinking water on hand.
- Do not walk or ride a bike in moving water above your knees.